Toothpaste & Pasta

FAITH AND FOOD FOR THE FAMILY

Pete Townsend

kevin
mayhew

First published in 2003 by
KEVIN MAYHEW LTD
Buxhall, Stowmarket, Suffolk, IP14 3BW
E-mail: info@kevinmayhewltd.com

© 2003 Pete Townsend

The right of Pete Townsend to be identified
as the author of this work has been asserted
by him in accordance with the Copyright, Designs
and Patents Act, 1988.

No part of this publication may be reproduced,
stored in a retrieval system, or transmitted, in
any form or by any means, electronic, mechanical,
photocopying, recording or otherwise, without
the prior written permission of the publisher.

All rights reserved.

9 8 7 6 5 4 3 2 1 0

ISBN 1 84417 012 8
Catalogue No. 1500562

Cover design by Angela Selfe
Edited and typeset by Elisabeth Bates
Printed and bound in Great Britain

Contents

Acknowledgements — 6
Introduction — 7

Baby Blues — 9
To boldly go ... — 11
The arrival! — 13
Tears — 16
Heavy! — 17
Bits and pieces — 19
Mumbles — 22
In awe — 24
Design flaw? — 26
The cement mixer — 28
Slam dunk — 32
Ouch! — 34
Playing choo-choo — 37

Toddler Terrors — 41
Wax rainbow — 43
If I ever ... — 46
Shoes — 51
Relatives — 54
Grand barney — 58
Zoology for infants? — 60
Wooden it be nice! — 64
Help ... — 66
Give me a break — 66

Nursery Nightmares — 69
First-day blues — 71
Myths, legends and suchlike — 74
Barking mad — 75
Cheers — 79
Transmogrification! — 79
Bugs and stuff — 83
Toothpaste murals — 84

Primary Pranks — 87
Scary teachers — 89
Thugs and mugs — 92
Education sucks — 93
The dentist — 97
Origin of the species — 98
Brussels sprouts and pasta — 100

Secondary Scares — 103
Hormone hell — 105
Is this music? — 108
It's life, Lord! — 110
Does it add up? — 111
Perhaps? — 113
The evolutionary grunt — 115
Life, the universe and growing up — 117

Recipes

Ratatouille	15
Pasta Platter	21
Potato and Leek Bake	31
Spicy Mushroom Topper	40
Crusty Vegetable Pie	49
Herb and Tomato Concoction	57
Cheesy, Spicy, Fruity Peaches!	63
Fruit and Nut Chocolate Extravaganza	73
Stir-fried Tofu with Peanut and Spring Onion Sauce	78
Butter Bean Salad	82
Tagliatelle with Courgettes and Crème Fraiche	91
Pear Tarts	96
Prawns in Tomato Sauce	102
Coconut Pyramids	107
Spicy Chick Peas with Ham	112
Croissants Stuffed with Apple Puree and Yoghurt	119

Acknowledgements

To all those who have looked at a newly born baby and said 'Ah, goo!' and to those who have looked at their latest culinary creation and said 'Ah goo!', this book is for you.

In particular, I would like to say a huge 'cheers' to my good friends Jane and Ed, with whom I have experienced many a happy meal and conversation. To Nig and Carol, whose friendship is as hearty as apple pie and custard. To Billy and Sharon whose own lives are an inspiration to all they meet: thanks.

And to Ruth, my love and best mate.

Introduction

Almost everything we come into contact with carries some form of warning. For instance, the instructions on a box containing a blowtorch read: 'Not to be used for drying hair'! Or, the instructions on the top rung of an aluminium ladder: 'STOP! This is the last rung'. Further guidance for our health and safety include a hairdryer with the warning: 'Do not use while sleeping', and the following hint found on the packaging for an iron: 'Do not iron clothes on body'. Such helpful hints and tips only go to show that people care about staying healthy, wealthy and wise! How else would you explain the amazingly considerate instructions found on the packaging for curling tongs: 'For external use only'!

With so much useful guidance around, you'd think that someone, somewhere, would take the time to provide just the tiniest hint that having children can cause serious drain bamage!

Having children seems to imply that we give no thought towards our health, income or sanity! It would be frightening to estimate the total amount of hours we've spent deprived of sleep, or adding up the cost of keeping our little bundles of joy in nappies or, more worrying, the number of times we've suddenly stopped in the street, pointed excitedly and exclaimed: 'Ooh, look at the big, red pap-pap. Brooom, brooom', only to discover that our intended audience is at home and we're surrounded by a crowd of bemused grown-ups!

If you're nodding as you read this, then you know the symptoms well. If you have a puzzled expression on your face, and are wondering what on earth this is about, be warned! It will not be long before you understand only too well.

The following thoughts, reflections and prayers are just some of the experiences that we will become familiar with during our journey through the parental swamp. There are five sections, starting with 'Baby Blues', stumbling into 'Toddler Terrors', bumping into 'Nursery Nightmares', falling foul of 'Primary Pranks', before we get the 'Secondary Scares'.

Scattered throughout the journey are quick and easy recipes to help nourish you along the way. They are not planned to take account of calorific yield or nutritional value, nor are they designed to help you host a dinner party. The recipes are simply there to enable you to grab a quick snack, indulge yourself or get something down the children's necks before they eat the furniture!

The book is here to let you know that you're not alone on the meandering track of parenthood. There are no 'dishy' pictures of the food. They will only make the book expensive and you'll only end up complaining that your attempts at the recipes look nothing like the pictures! Be creative in all things, especially your prayers!

You can dip in anywhere that takes your fancy, particularly the foody bits. Whatever you choose, enjoy. Just before I go, an important piece of advice found on a pushchair: 'Warning! Please remove child before folding.' Nuff said.

BABY BLUES

What with the antenatal bit (the uncertainty and fear of the unknown), and the postnatal bit (with the certainty that your fears of the unknown were totally justified), bringing a life into the world exposes us to the whole realm of emotions, as well as the feeling of being absolutely incompetent in handling a lump of soggy humanity. The excitement and wonder soon turn to bewilderment as we struggle to understand the intricacies of disposable nappies. There's a whole new universe of parenthood to explore and none of the DIY manuals appear to be written in a language any of us can comprehend. At times like these, a few heartfelt chats with God might just help us to realise that we are not alone . . .

To boldly go...

Well, Lord,
    here we are, this is it.
Boldly going into the vast unknown,
    exploring new life forms,
        experiencing the awakening of long-dormant senses.
This is it!
The anticipated event,
    the pinnacle of union,
        the ultimate ambition of humankind.

This whole journey, Lord,
    has been planned with meticulous care.
Every detail,
    every eventuality,
    every possibility,
    has been considered, pondered, rationalised
    and discussed thoroughly.
Even when the journey was nothing more
    than an impulse,
    a stirring neuron,
    a mere twinkle in our eyes,
    a sort of silly smirk on our faces.
But we knew, Lord,
    that together,
    hand in hand,
    we were standing on the edge of our known world,
    looking forward, together,
    at the dawning of a new age.
A new beginning.

This, Lord, is a journey that will stretch our imagination,
    provide challenges beyond our comprehension.
It feels awesome.
The anticipation,
    the excitement,
    the exhilaration.
It's almost too difficult to contain our emotions.
One minute it feels like a dream,
    as if it will never happen.
The next moment,
    the feeling of panic attacks.
We're not ready for this.
Nothing's sorted,
    nothing's prepared.
There's so much left to do,
    things to buy,
    people to inform,
    books to read,
    people to consult,
    pamphlets to digest.
More time, we need more time.
And then, Lord,
    slowly, very slowly,
    the sense of wonder returns.
So, the bag's packed,
    the 'To do' list is checked off,
    the plans are complete,
    tests and trial runs have been done and run.
And now, we await the final phase,
    the countdown,

preparing ourselves for the encounter with a new life-form.
Lord, here, on Planet Earth,
   you might have guessed,
      that we're really looking forward,
         to the birth of our baby.

The arrival!

Lord,
   nothing, absolutely nothing could have prepared me for this.
One moment everything is normal (whatever that is),
   and the next... kapow!
The room is filled with ear-shattering screams
   as this new life forces itself into the world.

Help! Lord,
   who's in control?
I'm certainly not.
I seem to be a bystander, a mere spectator.
I don't feel in control of my legs any more;
   and I don't think that my wife knows where she left her legs last,
   or whether she's given up ownership of them completely.

Lord, what am I doing here?
My wife wanted me to be here,
   I wanted me to be here!
But now I'm here, I feel like a spare part.
No matter where I stand I feel in someone's way.

'Move here, move there. No! stand over there.
Just move to one side, please. Standing room only.'
Hey! Hang on a minute. Who sold tickets to the main event?
Who are all these people?
They certainly weren't around at the beginning of this process,
   so why are they here now at the completion?

I dread to think what my wife thinks or feels at this moment;
   she's too intent on mistaking my thumb for the gas and air tube!
The look on her face pains me,
   and I think she might be feeling the occasional twinge
   as she struggles to eject this new life into the world.
(Somehow, Lord, the image of a camel and the eye of a needle
   come to mind at the moment.)

Just a minute, Lord,
   something is happening,
   stand by, I'll keep you posted
   and tell you as soon as I have any news . . .
Whoops! Wow! Neat catch, nurse!
Oh, Lord,
   you should see this, it's fantastic.
Everyone is in tears,
   or is that just the way I'm seeing things
   through my own downpour?
Get back to you, Lord, as soon as I can.

Ratatouille

So much has been going on that you just might have forgotten (in between buying nappies, the essential dummy, baby clothes, and other assorted paraphernalia that assaults the eyeballs) to buy a few other important items such as food. This recipe will allow you to grab whatever bits and pieces of vegetables you can find to stop yourself wasting away!

Ingredients (serves about 4 people)

- 1 tablespoon olive oil
- 1 large onion, chopped coarsely
- 1-2 cloves garlic, finely chopped
- Large can chopped tomatoes
- 1 tablespoon tomato puree
- 2-3 peppers, diced
- Handful mixed herbs
- 6 courgettes, sliced
- Salt and pepper

1. Heat the oil in a pan and fry the onions and garlic for a couple of minutes.
2. Add the courgettes and peppers and cook for 8-10 minutes.
3. Put the tomatoes, herbs and tomato puree in with the rest of the mixture. Cook for a further 10 minutes.
4. Season with the salt and pepper and serve.

You can add any other vegetables to the mixture that might be lurking around the kitchen. Aubergines, cubed, or sliced carrots are a neat addition, as is roughly chopped fennel or green beans. Be careful not to overcook the mixture as this will require you to rename the dish 'Ratastewie'!

Tears

Just a quick chat, Lord.
You know that tears thing I mentioned earlier?
Can I ask you about that?
You see, I'm a touch mixed up here.
I'm happy, no doubt about that,
    but I'm also angry,
        in fact I'm really angry.
Why?
You tell me.
What's all this pain bit for?
Why is something so wonderful, so awesome,
    wrapped up in a bucket load of pain?

Lord, I don't want to be angry at this time,
    especially not with you.
But I can't get my head around the pain bit.
Nothing personal,
    it's just that I can't cope with this very well.
You may have noticed that I turn away
    when there's anything in the least pain-inducing on TV.
The first hint of a drop of blood
    and I become all helpful,
    offering to go and make a pot of tea,
    in fact I insist on going and making a pot of tea.
So, as you can understand,
    I'm finding this something less than easy.
Speak to you later,
I'm off to find an aspirin.

Heavy!

Lord,
>this has got to be the most 'heavy' moment of my life
(7 pounds 6 ounces or, to be more precise, 3.34 kilos in new money).

Wow! Wahey!! . . . It's a boy!
This is the most awesome, absolutely gob-smacking,
>inspiring and exceptionally frightening time
of my whole residency on Planet Earth.

And, you might like to know,
>the aspirin worked, and I'm feeling loads better, thanks.

Lord,
>are you really sure about entrusting this thing,
this item of humanity, to us?

What are we supposed to do now?
>(apart from attempting to get some sleep;
I'm exhausted and I think my co-conspirator in all of this
is a touch tired too!)

Aren't there any labels or stuff to go with it?
Which way up does it go?
How does it work?
Does it need batteries?
What do you feed it with?

Just before you start to panic, Lord
>(or should that read: 'before *I* start to panic, Lord . . .'),
I'd like to say that I'm really quite impressed
with this parenthood thing
(and I very much enjoyed the creating bit!),

but, I do think that you should include an owner's guide,
    a sort of manual for the bemused parent.
Shouldn't there be a sort of guidance thing for first-time owners?
Let's face it,
    I couldn't just stroll down the road with a loaded cheque-book,
    buy the first car I see and drive it away
    if I hadn't passed my driving-test!
Not only that,
    shouldn't I be insured as well,
    you know, against accidents –
    bumping into people with an uncoordinated pushchair –
    or third-party insurance
    for those moments when the little gurgling bundle
    ejects pints of partially digested milk feed
    over some unsuspecting baby bouncer?
But no!
A wink and a smile and several months later,
    we find ourselves in charge of an organic entity
    that could go haywire at the slightest hint of an E-number.

OK, Lord,
    I suppose we'll have to learn the hard way.
We can give it a bit of a test run,
    tinker about with it,
    try a few modifications and, hopefully,
    it'll be fine-tuned enough, given time, to become
    a fully fledged member of the human race.
Oh, by the way, we might need a bit of a hand now and again.
Just thought we'd let you know.
Cheers.

Bits and pieces

Lord,
    you know how people always gather around a baby
    and coo a lot and generally make noises that make you
    want to find a paper bag
    to contain your feelings!
Well, I was just wondering about a few things.
When someone says,
    'Oh, look, isn't it sweet, he's got Uncle Gerald's nose,
    and Aunt Sophie's ears',
    it causes me to think
    (and not just about what are Uncle Gerald and Aunt Sophie doing
    now that they've given up part of their anatomy for a good cause),
    and it just made me remember,
    that bit immediately after the birth,
    when the nurse
    lays the baby on a blanket,
    looks admiringly,
    and then does an inventory check
    of all its bits and pieces.

Lord, at the time,
    I thought nothing of it,
    apart from a quick thanks to you,
    for the safe delivery,
    and that we're all OK.
But, now,
    I pause
    and wonder;

'Would I still love our baby,
   if it had more, or less, than it should have?'
Would it be any less a human being,
   due all the love and care that it deserves?
Could I deprive it of emotion,
   of comfort,
   of security,
   just because it didn't meet all the requirements
   of the baby magazine pictures?
There, with all its integrity,
   its feelings and developing personality,
   is a human
   desperately in need
   of a loving embrace.
What choice is there?

Pasta Platter

Ingredients (serves about 3-4)
225g/8oz penne pasta
6 medium sized tomatoes, chopped
4 courgettes, sliced
1 tablespoon of olive oil
50g/2oz pitted black olives, drained and chopped
400g/14oz can mixed beans, drained
Pepper

Dressing:
2 tablespoons tomato puree
A generous glug white/red wine
2 tablespoons fromage frais or unsweetened yoghurt
1 tablespoon dark brown sugar
Herbs: either a handful of fresh, chopped basil or a teaspoon of dried basil/oregano

1. Cook the penne pasta in boiling water according to the instructions on the packet. Do not overcook the pasta as it will continue cooking with the other ingredients.
2. Drain the pasta and return it to the pan. Stir in the olive oil, chopped tomatoes and beans. Continue to heat gently for about 5-6 minutes.
3. Add the courgettes and cook for a further 2-3 minutes.
4. Spoon the mixture onto a large plate or platter, add the olives and a sprinkling of ground pepper.
5. To make the dressing, mix all the ingredients together and drizzle over the vegetables and pasta.

You can vary the ingredients by adding a 225g/8oz can of tuna, drained and flaked in with the vegetables, or finely chopped pieces of bacon which has been cooked separately.

Mumbles

'Mmmrrmm...'
Lord, sorry for mumbling.
You see, it's a bit difficult
   to talk properly,
     owing to this extremely fat bottom lip.
It hurts like... well,
   I'm sure you can guess.

Do you know,
   it wouldn't have happened,
   the fat lip bit, not the baby thing,
   if the door hadn't been slightly open,
   on account of it not being shut,
   which it usually is,
   to keep out the vibrant slumbers
   of the new addition to the family.

Lord,
   why is it that these
   sighs, gurgles, coos, and moves
   sound so lovable
   in the bright light of day, but
   sound like an orchestra
   of ever-so-slightly
   uncoordinated hippos
   in the quiet darkness
   of the small hours?

Anyway, Lord,
   this embrace of the door
   with my sleep-sodden facial features,
   was a surprise to me,
   because I can't quite remember
   whether I left the door open
   on one of my previous visits
   to the inner sanctum of babyhood
   (I gave up counting after the seventh trip)
   or whether I closed the door
   and it decided to remain partly open
   to make it easier to dodge out of the way
   when a cranky figure
   lurched and fumbled its way
   towards the demanding sounds.

It certainly wasn't a result of getting out of bed too quickly.
That's impossible at the moment,
   and altogether tricky,
   with my sprained ankle
   (nasty encounter with a recently divested nappy ... darkness = visibility problem = difficult foot positioning = squelch, slip, OW!)
   and, I probably would have seen that the door was ajar,
   if my vision wasn't impaired
   by a swollen eye
   (baby and erratic head movements = fatherly cuddle = infant impact = Wham! Ouch! = cold compress on eye).

Still, the little bundle is fast asleep again now ... until the next time.
I don't know how to say how grateful we are,

other than thanks.
And now, Lord,
   my apologies,
   but can I continue our conversation
   when I next make my nightly perambulation,
   but I need to concentrate on getting back to my bed . . . safely.
Now, where's that door lurking?

In awe

Lord,
   I stand in awe of you:
   your infinite wisdom knows no limits,
Your love is without boundaries.
Your creation is majestic.
The sky alone gives a glimpse
   of your smile,
   while the Earth below
   reassures us of your creative might.
The mountains,
   in the stillness of dawn's breathy light,
   stand as a visual challenge
   to all who would tread
   the summits.

Lord,
   the trees,
   with their roots
   firmly gripping the earth,

stand proud, heads held high,
with their foliage
a verdant crown.

The flowers,
    which scent the air,
    lift the senses
    and transport the mind
    into a heady atmosphere
    of your presence.

Lord,
    your omnipotence,
    your creative omniscience,
    is beyond comprehension.
So,
    having realised how great you are,
    how understanding and loving,
    how powerful and majestic,
    nothing out of your control,
    nothing out of your reach,
    could you please tell me one,
    just one, simple thing,
    'How on earth do I stop this little bundle of life
    from screaming
    its head off?'

Design flaw?

You must be joking here,
  this can't be for real.
I mean, just take a look
  at this mess!
I don't know whether to
  mop up, wipe up or use
  a bucket and spade!

Now, I don't want to appear
  critical of you as the Creator and all that,
  but I think there might be
  just a minor
  design flaw here!

I know, I know,
  it's 3 in the morning
  and everything takes on
  nightmarish proportions,
  but this outweighs
  (quite literally)
  my worst nightmare scenario . . . big time.

It's like some kind
  of unnatural phenomenon.
Just how could such a small container
  hold so much?
Dr Who's Tardis has nothing on this.
(Just in case you were busy at the time,

    Dr Who was a hand-knitted time-traveller
    who had a few run-ins with bits of latex and tin.)
Where was I?
Yuck! As if I didn't know.
Don't get me wrong, Lord,
    I don't mind doing my bit and all that,
    it's a part of this parenthood gig,
    it's a partnership thing,
    this baby business,
    but even at a ratio of 2:1
    the odds seem stacked heavily in the baby's favour.

Just think,
    humankind has travelled in space
    (not as far as Dr Who, but we're getting there . . .
    unless it all gets privatised),
    we've split the atom – big mistake as splitting the atom
    has gone on to split lots of other, more tangible, objects ever since,
    we've messed around with genetics
    and modified anything that'll
    stand still long enough,
    yet, with all this technical know-how,
    we still can't invent
    a disposable nappy
    that doesn't work on the self-emptying principle,
    or doesn't explode
    the moment you pull at the sticky tabs.
Sorry to moan,
    but it's not like this happens once or twice a week,
    this goes on at least three times a day!

Oh well,
    nothing for it
    but to wrap another disposable container (ha, ha!)
    around the little mite.
Amazing things,
    these miniature humans
    that still need a bit of organic adjustment here and there.
Still, Lord,
    it's a small hassle
    in the great scheme of things.
Thanks for being there.
Must go,
    I need a shower.

The cement mixer

Lord,
    apologies for my appearance,
    but needs must, and all that.
I know that I look something like
    a cross between a deep-sea diver and a sewage technician.
However,
    when you're faced with the explosive force
    of this sweet little monster
    then anyone and everyone
    would take the necessary precautions
    to prevent being pebble-dashed
    with food debris.

I must admit, Lord,
    I find it somewhat baffling
    that,
    given the limited mobility and general inability
    of our offspring
    to actually escape mealtimes,
    he seems to have an excellent range of tactics
    for avoiding whatever morsels of food
    that, somehow, don't appeal to his sense of
    culinary adventure.

I've mashed and pureed,
    squashed and mushed
    until my arms ache
    and my head hurts,
    but he still manages to find
    the slightest lump,
    the most minute piece of grit-sized food
    and eject it with the force and precision of a laser-guided missile.

Lord,
    I'm sure that Einstein
    would have been able to explain it all,
    but I find it totally bemusing
    that what should take 20 minutes
    seems to last for an hour, at least.
Relativity doesn't go any way to explaining
    the devious infant twist
    upon time.

TOOTHPASTE AND PASTA

Lord,
    if we had known, beforehand,
    the level and intensity
    of this psychological warfare
    that goes on between parent and infant,
    then I might, just might, have suggested
    getting a dog instead!
But,
    this is our lot,
    and we mustn't grumble
    (who am I fooling?),
    and somehow, some way
    I'm going to bribe, cajole,
    cheat, sneak, trick and coax
    every last grain of food
    into this male child
    if it's the last thing I ever do.
Hang on, though,
    this chocolate pudding stuff
    tastes half decent.
Now, how about one spoon for him,
    and two for me (got to help out, haven't I?).
Another two for me and,
    whoops! He doesn't want his,
    I'll have it.
Two more for me and,
    sorry, Lord,
    speak to you later,
    my mouth is a bit full at the moment.

Potato and Leek Bake

Ingredients (serves 4)

500g/1lb potatoes, sliced
250ml/½-pint bechamel sauce
Salt and pepper

500g/1lb leeks, washed and sliced
Nutmeg

1. Cook the potatoes in boiling water for about 5 minutes and then drain.
2. Cook the leeks in boiling water for approximately 4 minutes and drain.
3. In a greased, ovenproof dish, mix in half of the potatoes and leeks, season and add the remainder of the potatoes and leeks.
4. Pour over the bechamel sauce. Grate some nutmeg over the mixture.
5. Bake for 30 minutes at Gas Mark 5.

Bechamel sauce:
125ml/½-pint milk
25g/1oz plain flour

25g/1oz margarine

1. Melt the margarine in a saucepan.
2. Add the flour and cook for one minute.
3. Gradually add the milk and stir.
4. Allow the mixture to slowly come to the boil, stirring continuously.

You might like to add some grated cheese to the sauce or add a tablespoon of Dijon mustard.

Slam dunk

Just thought you'd like to know, Lord,
  that we're just about to do the Church bit,
  and get the young sprog,
  dressed in his Sunday best,
  sprinkled with water,
  and generally
  advertise the fact
  that we're really chuffed
  with our lad.

He's just a bit great.
He smiles and giggles,
  chortles and grins,
  and regularly laughs his gums off.
It's brilliant when he snuggles into your shoulder,
  or bounces merrily on your knee and . . .
Oh, yeah, the bouncing thing.
I should have known better.
Recently ingested food and bouncing
  are not a good combination.
It's never a pretty sight,
  having an action replay,
  in reverse,
  of the feeding event
  which took place
  only minutes before.
Never mind, the jeans should wash and,
  if the stain doesn't come out,

I could always dye them
   a vibrant shade of puce.

And that gets me thinking
   of dark, sleepless nights,
   feeding and burping
   (getting up in the night always makes me hungry
   and then gives me indigestion),
   changing nappies and singing snatches
   of tuneless nursery rhymes,
   in a futile attempt at inducing sleep
   throughout the house.

And another thing,
   whatever happened to quality time?
When we've finished dashing here and there,
   doing this and that,
   washing anything that stands still long enough, then
   those few seconds that are left
   are taken up
   with negotiating the stairs
   in search of a bed
   where we can lay ourselves down
   and reminisce of earlier times
   when sleep was a close friend
   and not some distant, illusive memory.

Is there an end to all this?
Is there a . . . wait a moment,
   if I carry on like this,

I might object to expressing my thanks
in front of so many other people,
who, let's be honest, only see the good bits
and might not appreciate
some of the more choice comments
that may escape from my lips.

So, Lord,
   we'll say thanks anyway,
   mainly because we're sure, or fairly sure,
   that the good bits will outweigh the not-so-good bits . . . possibly.

Ouch!

This is far from funny, Lord,
   I'm scared,
   and not at all confident that I can go through with this.
I'm not a wimp or anything
   you understand,
   but some things just get under my skin,
   and, in this case,
   actually do get under the skin.

Yeah, that's it,
   needles or, to be more precise, injections.
Whoever dreamt up a scheme
   where a grown-up
   shoves a great lump of metal into your
   soft, sensitive, fragile skin?

Another thing, Lord,
    are these chemicals,
        that are supposed to protect us,
        from all sorts of nasty things,
        not themselves responsible
        for lots of other nasty things?
We don't know who to believe.
We've read leaflets and books,
    talked to doctors and parents,
        and still those stories emerge
        of damages caused
        where the intention was
        to remove the threat of damage.

Now, neither of us is into gambling,
    but the odds seem to show
        that there is a greater risk
        of damage
        without immunisation,
        than with.
But, Lord,
    what if we, or rather, our son,
        draws the short straw?
Who's to blame?
Is there blame?
The intentions are honest
    and for the best,
        but that doesn't repair
        the damage done.

As I sit my son on my lap,
    I can't help but marvel at his life,
    a simple expression of love
    that has created a unique individual
    that is the sum total of ages past.
I turn my head,
    having made the choice
    to immunise.
For better or for worse,
    this is our decision.
He sits unsuspecting,
    intrigued by the object of potential hurt,
    while I hide my fear,
    my head in the sand of hopeful ignorance.

Lord, help us,
    to continually look to you.
Not that we pass the blame
    or weight of ignorance
    on to you,
    but that we thank you for each and every moment
    of this life, this responsibility,
    this commitment
    to life
    which we share.
Help us, Lord,
    to involve you
    in every way,
    in every step
    along this uncertain path of parenthood.

Playing choo-choo

'Here we go round the mulber...'
Ah, erm, hmm...
Sorry, Lord,
   bit of confusion creeping in here.
As you might expect,
   'She'll be comin' round the mountain when...'
Oops, another verbal slippage.
Where was I?
Oh, yeah,
   'Choo-choo. Choo-choo!'
Oh Lord, help.

My head's crammed full of nursery rhymes,
   and other strange, verbal utterances.
It's this baby job, you see.
I seem to spend half of my time talking
   in a language
     that appears to consist almost entirely of vowels,
     with the occasional consonant thrown in for decoration.
Quite frankly, Lord,
   it's embarrassing.
Show me an adult and I'm tongue-tied;
   show me a stubby little nappy-wrapped squawk-box
   and I can jabber away for hours.

Lord,
   there must be a simple way
   of conveniently switching between

'bibbish' (a language made up of vowels, dribble
and almost anything else that collects in a bib)
and 'dulltese' (everyday, sensible, adult inane chatter).
Whilst my outward appearance
may give the impression of an articulate,
and fully grown-up piece of tax fodder,
my open mouth betrays me every time.

For example,
and I know you're still having a giggle about this,
my short sojourn on a train last week
found me gazing,
as contentedly as the cows,
while frame after frame
of patchwork fields
skidded passed my window.
The scenes were everything
a baby-book illustrates.
A smile crept across my face while my mouth exclaimed:
'Aah, just look at the liddle moo-moos,
a chew, chewin' the grass while Old MacDonald...'
Several pairs of eyes alerted me to the fact
that I was describing the scenes
to my lunch-box which sat appreciatively next to me!
I decided to get off the train
three stops before I needed, to avoid the stomach-churning
embarrassment of sad nods,
and still the whole carriage waved to me
as the train pulled away,
leaving me standing

    like a lone prune
    in a bowl of cold custard.

Lord,
    my head really cannot cope with this.
I'm humming nursery rhymes all the time;
    I answer the phone with
    'Allo, and how are we today den?';
    my lunch-box contains
    yellow teddy yoghurts,
    jam-drenched rusks
    and juice cartons with jungle pictures
    all over them.
I wake up in the morning
    to find myself in the foetal position,
    with dribble on my chin
    and a great stubby thumb
    rammed firmly in my mouth!

So help me, Lord,
    before I become prematurely infantile,
    and I'm checking out the 4 x 4 buggies
    rather than MPVs!

Spicy Mushroom Topper

This is a real treat for those moments when you feel as if you've been squeezed dry by everyone and everything! A little bit of preparation, a quick dash of heat and your mouth will thank you for hours afterwards.

Ingredients (serves 4)
1 tablespoon olive oil
400g/14oz mushrooms, quartered
1 tablespoon mixed herbs
Grated cheese
3 cloves garlic, chopped finely
10 slices of baguette
1 teaspoon garam masala

1. Heat the olive oil in a frying pan, add the garlic and garam masala. Cook for about 20 seconds.
2. Add the mushrooms and cook for approximately 6 minutes.
3. Toast the slices of baguette on one side only. Once one side is toasted, turn over and brush the other side lightly with olive oil, and toast.
4. Throw the herbs into the mushrooms and stir.
5. Spoon the mushroom mixture over the toast. Sprinkle the cheese over the mushrooms and eat immediately.

TODDLER TERRORS

These are those years when the emerging psychopath . . . er, sorry, I mean our darling little creation, crawls from babyhood into something that totters around causing panic. It's not so much the 'ah' stage as the 'aaargh!' stage.

Wax rainbow

Lord,
    may I just say
    how completely amazed I am
    at your creation of life.
The results are truly incredible,
    a riot of colour
    against the nondescript backwash
    of magnolia walls.

Really, Lord,
    I am gobsmacked at this wonder of life,
    the outwardly simple
    disguising a complexity of nature.
It's clever, Lord,
    the way things literally work themselves through.
And,
    just in case you were wondering
    what I'm on about,
    let me explain.

I thought that a simple,
    creative act
    might develop our little lad's appreciation
    of art,
    along with the contrast and co-ordination
    of colour,
    together with the combination of subtle shades
    forming a visual feast for the eye.

But,
    as with all things,
    my adult brain
    failed to comprehend the most simple,
    the blindingly obvious,
    the true nature
    of a toddler.
So, rather than produce
    a piece of artwork
    worthy of exhibition
    in a gallery of abstract impressionism,
    our little bundle of joy
    ripped up the lovely blank piece of paper,
    tipped all the wax crayons onto the floor,
    and,
    in a most co-ordinated manner,
    proceeded to eat his way through
    the entire wax rainbow.

Now,
    as you might expect,
    my momentary panic
    (please ignore my wife, I didn't get hysterical
    or even remotely flustered, and anyway,
    my repeated dialling of the emergency services
    simply keeps them on their toes, you know, for a real emergency)
    soon found something positive to focus on
    as I attempted to hook bits of paper and crayon
    out of his mouth.
To me, this was the obvious thing to do

and, as I've already said,
the most obvious of actions
doesn't always register the consequences.
The resulting pool of vomit
neatly sinking into the textured carpet
basically informed me
that the crayons were made in China,
and that our son had eaten
peas and carrots for breakfast!
(no, I can't work that one out either).

As we put our bundle of joy to bed,
I do remember asking you
to make sure he slept well,
and that you'd keep him safe and well.
Your response,
or way of working things out,
certainly made an impression
when we changed his nappy the next morning.
What a sight,
a myriad of colourful flecks,
a scene worthy of a comment
by any eminent art critic.
So, thanks, Lord,
for seeing us through
(and the crayon bit through as well)
a situation that was initially frightening,
and ultimately enlightening,
but which helped us to marvel at your creation
and marvel at the ingenuity of toddlers,

along with a certain lesson in parenthood,
that it doesn't always pay
to critically evaluate every action,
but often,
just let him have fun,
and a wax-free diet in future.

If I ever . . .

Lord,
    if I ever, even remotely
    mention any words
    such as: great, brill, wow, smart, terrific,
    or words with a sort of similar meaning,
    then you have my permission
    to peg out my tongue,
    slap raspberry jam all over it,
    and let the ants have a picnic!

I just can't believe what I'm almost seeing.
One moment our nappy-wrapped cherub
    is sitting playing quietly with his menagerie of soft toys,
    and then,
    a millisecond later,
    he's leading a stampede of furry animals
    towards a watering hole
    located in the kitchen!

How did he get there?

TODDLER TERRORS

From where he was playing to the kitchen
   is three rooms away!
Lord, is there something you're not telling us?
You know,
   like there's a turbo boost switch
     whose location is known only to our little whirlwind.

This mini revelation
   has got us in a sweat.
How do we know when he's going to hit warp 6?
Do we get a warning,
   or do we wait for the dust to settle
   and assess the damage then?
How can we warn innocent people?
One second they may be sitting on the sofa
   enjoying a nice cup of tea,
   and the next,
   dripping head-to-toe,
   in brown liquid
   and wondering why the weather forecast
   made no mention of a cyclone
   coming their way!

Lord,
   can you imagine
   strapping him into his buggy
   at the precise moment that his metabolism
   mimics nuclear fusion?
He'll be zooming down the High Street,
   straps straining,

buggy glowing white-hot,
with a parent
grimly holding on for dear life
as the 'G-force' distorts the ageing face
causing the worry lines to reappear at the back of the head!
And, this is the most frightening thing of all,
   he hasn't even learnt to walk yet!

OK, Lord,
   this is the point where we need help . . . big time.
In your infinite wisdom,
   you have allowed us
   to combine our genes
   to create a trainee human
   whose predilection for matter-transfer
   baffles scientists
   but is elementary for toddlers.
Forget the 'Whys?', Lord,
   please just tell us the 'How?'

Sincerely begging,
   I remain,
   stationary, in one place,
   your totally confused
   example of the adult species.

Crusty Vegetable Pie

This is a simple dish with an interesting variation. You can serve this with either jacket potato, mashed potato or grab some oven chips out of the freezer! Enjoy.

Ingredients (serves 4-6)
750g/1½lb mixed vegetables (carrots, peppers, courgettes, mushrooms, peas, sweetcorn and broccoli), chopped or sliced, but I'd leave the peas and sweetcorn as they are!
300g/12oz potatoes, cubed
300ml/½-pint coconut milk
100g/4oz cheese
150g/6oz shortcrust pastry
3 tablespoons cornflour
2 tablespoons olive oil
Salt and pepper

Make the pastry first. To do this you need:
110g/4oz plain flour
50g/2oz margarine
A pinch of salt
Water to mix

1. Sift the flour and salt into a large mixing bowl.
2. Rub in the margarine with your finger-tips until the mixture starts to become crumbly.
3. Add a little water and, using a wooden spoon, carefully mix all the ingredients together until you get a ball of dough that doesn't stick to the bowl.
4. Put the pastry into a polythene bag and place it in the fridge for about 20 minutes.

The vegetables:
1. Preheat the oven to 200°C/Gas Mark 6.
2. Place the mixed vegetables into a large pan of boiling water and cook until just tender

3. In a separate pan, cook the potatoes.
4. Drain all the vegetables and place them into a large ovenproof dish.
5. Mix the cornflour and coconut milk together. Cook gently in a small saucepan, stirring continually until the mixture begins to thicken. Stir in the grated cheese and season.
6. Pour the sauce over the vegetables.
7. Remove the pastry from the fridge, roll out the pastry on a floured surface until it's a little larger than the pie dish. Drape the pastry over the dish and firm the edges with your thumb or, if you want to be fancy, press a fork (either end!) around the edges of the pastry. You can glaze the pastry with a drop of milk or beaten egg.
8. Bake for approximately 20 minutes or until the pastry has a neat golden colour.

Shoes

I didn't mean to do it,
    honest, Lord.
I simply couldn't help myself.
If it had been left up to me,
    I'd have turned my back and walked away,
    straight up, I would have done.
But, well,
    she thought the shoes were just what should adorn
    every toddler's feet.

I ask you,
Have you seen the price of these things?
There's hardly anything to them.
It's just a few small pieces of leather,
    a couple of bits of metal,
    a touch of coloured thread,
    some glue,
    stitch here, stitch there
    and hey presto!
    a pair of shoes ready for scuffing along the floor.

All I asked was, '*How* much?'
A simple question,
    emphasised with a gesture
    at the flickering display of numbers
    signalling that yet another sucker
    was just about to be parted from a great wad of sweat-money.

TOOTHPASTE AND PASTA

It might have been the question,
   the gesture,
   or combination of the two,
   but now the assistant isn't speaking to me,
   my wife isn't speaking to me,
   the other shoppers are 'tutting' and making sucking noises
   with their indignant lips.

But,
   is it so wrong
   to question the cost
   and make a stand for all
   sleep-deprived parents everywhere?

I know my wife thinks the same as me,
   her eyes gave her away,
   but she appears to be totally appalled
   that I should voice our concern
   so loudly,
   and vigorously,
   so obviously,
   in front of all those people,
   some of whom just might know us!

Oh well,
   in the great scheme of things
   it's not actually so much to pay,
   for a bit of peace and quiet,
   recognition that I exist.

So,
   as I said,
   I didn't mean to do it,
   that is,
   neither pay through the nose for a miniature pair of shoes,
   or cause the declaration
   of retail hostilities
   between the innocent shopper (me!)
   and the assembled forces of commerce
   (including the local Mothers' Union).

Lord,
   I don't understand this.
What a skip-load of hassle,
   over a bit of fabric and leather,
   when our little lad
   can't even walk yet!
But who am I to grumble?
Who am I to complain?
I just want to avoid
   another look of disdain!
   (it must be something he inherited from his mum!).

Relatives

Lord,
   relatively speaking,
   I stand in absolute amazement
   at your sense of humour.

Having a laugh
   must have been top of your list
   when you sketched out the basic idea
   for creating human beings.

Most of all,
   I think you might have had
   a real celestial hoot
   when you came up with the idea
   of 'relatives'.

You must have known
   the mayhem relatives would cause
   when a new addition
   arrived within the family.

The sight of a miracle
   of new life
   sends every female relative
   into a frenzy
   of incomprehensible speech,
   while all the males
   just nod knowingly,

pretending to have this
bringing-up-kids business sussed,
when, in actual fact,
they have no idea
what's what, what's where,
or how their kids
ever grew up in the first place!

A new member of the family
   appears to give everyone
   the right to act as stupid
   as you can imagine.
Aunts cooing and gooing,
   uncles pulling faces
   with wide-open mouths,
   to reveal enough internal pipe-work
   to make a plumber
   rub his hands in delight.

Grandparents have a special role,
   which includes,
   as a matter of priority,
   the right to do everything and anything,
   with their grandchild,
   which they would never have done,
   or allowed,
   with you.
Sweets before meals,
   dribbling on the best furniture,
   juggling with the best ornaments,

swinging the cat around by its tail.
All of these would have earned us
   severe words,
   isolation in our bedroom,
   no treats,
   no sweets,
   and certainly no laughs.
But, for their grandchild,
   anything goes,
   while the grandparents smile,
   nod their heads
   and say what a delight their grandchild is!

I don't know whether
   all of this is making any sense to you, Lord,
But it means a lot to me.
I'm trying to do the right things
   only to see grandparents
   ride roughshod over everything,
   making us look like authoritarian ogres
   who are about as much fun
   as a sawdust sandwich.

I don't understand it, Lord,
   I don't find it amusing,
   but I'm sure you're having a giggle,
   at our discomfiture.
Still, perhaps we should have a giggle ourselves
   before we start ripping the wallpaper off the walls
   in frustration.

Herb and Tomato Concoction

A very simple soup that tastes superb served hot with chunks of fresh bread. Alternatively, you could serve this cold during the summer; whatever takes your fancy, really.

Ingredients (serves 4)

3 tablespoons olive oil	2 large onions, finely chopped
2 cloves garlic	6-8 large tomatoes, roughly chopped
1 teaspoon basil	1 teaspoon thyme
1 teaspoon coriander	300ml/½-pint milk
300ml/½-pint water	Black pepper
125ml/¼-pint single cream	

1. Heat the olive oil in a pan.
2. Cook the onions until lightly browned.
3. Add the tomatoes and cook for a further 3-4 minutes.
4. Stir in the milk and water, gradually add the herbs and stir.
5. Continue to heat the ingredients for another 12-15 minutes.
6. Puree the soup in a blender.
7. Return the soup to the pan and reheat for approximately 5 minutes.
8. Serve the soup in bowls. Pour a swirl of the cream into each bowl of soup and garnish with a sprinkling of basil.

Grand barney

Lord,
    I've just had a right royal barney
    with my dad.
I admit,
    it all got a bit out of hand,
    I'm sorry to say.
I suppose it's been building up for a while now.
I've bitten my lip,
    kept quiet,
    when all my instincts wanted to shout out
    in indignation.

I feel as if I've had
    my feet kicked from underneath me.
I've feel as if I've been made to look a clown,
    a figure to laugh at,
    when all I wanted to do was to act like a real dad.
But what am I expected to do
    when my own dad,
    someone I've grown to respect,
    doesn't behave like the dad he was
    when I was a kid?

All I did was to walk into the kitchen
    look at the wall-to-wall carpet of toys
    and, in the light of health and safety at home,
    suggest that the toys
    constituted a health hazard.

I didn't happen to see
   that my dad was busily
   recreating the leaning Tower of Pisa
   out of Duplo bricks
   in the middle of the kitchen floor,
   while his grandson
   was loading the washing-machine
   with empty yoghurt pots
   and every plastic animal from his toy ark.

Now, I suppose I must ask, Lord,
   but who's doing the kiddy bit here?
Or, are both of them acting like yoghurt pots?
All I got out of my dad was a sharp, 'He's not doing any harm,'
   while I enquired whether he was referring to his grandson
   or himself.

Things did get a bit heated,
   and in between the 'grow up', 'loosen up' and 'shut up!'
   we both got our ears singed
   when the object of our argument
   was rescued just before his feet disappeared entirely
   into the washing machine.
Grandma was furious
   as she nestled her grandson in her protective arms.
Dad's mime of bread being toasted
   from the heat of his wife's breath
   was just a bit too much
   for an angry wife,
   an annoyed mother

and a protective grandmother.
Dad was banished to the garden shed,
   while I had to endure the confines
   of my son's bedroom.

Sometime later
   (I haven't got the hang of this kiddie clock, with monkeys
   and ticking bananas, so I can't give an exact time),
   Dad and I were allowed out to discuss our behaviour!
I mumbled something about learning to be a dad,
   while Dad muttered something about learning to be a grandad.
Neither of us is sure about how we are supposed to act,
   or behave!
And, if you think about it,
   if we haven't a clue
   about this whole grown-up business,
   what kind of role model
   are we for my son?
Don't answer that,
   we might not appreciate the answer!

Zoology for infants!

Lord,
   I thought I'd dealt with most things.
I was even quite proud of the fact
   that I hardly blinked
   when recently swallowed food, ejected with tremendous force,

TODDLER TERRORS

    made an interesting pattern
    on my freshly ironed jeans.
And, you may have noticed,
    that I have an amazing capacity to hold my breath
    while changing a nappy
    that bears no resemblance to the last meal!
Even better,
    I barely flinched at the last round of immunisation jabs
    (OK, OK, I fainted, but that doesn't count).
But, Lord, this latest incident,
    it's, well, sort of totally off the wall.
Or, to be more precise,
    totally off the floor.

In one of those rare moments,
    when there's time to daydream,
    and ponder on life's mysteries,
    I took the time to gaze out of the window
    to admire the wonder of nature,
    and, there in all it's gooey, wriggly, slimy, yucky glory,
    was a typical example of your creative endeavour.
A snail twitched vainly,
    its head just poking out from the vice-like grip
    of my son's mouth!

Even I was amazed at the speed
    at which I erupted into the great outdoors,
    to prise an innocent creature
    from the jaws of death!
My son, giggling at his father's contorted face,

and panic-laden voice,
thought the antiseptic wipes
and torrents of water down his throat
were all part of the game,
which caused him to chuckle, hiccup and chortle
in pure ignorance of the fact
that he'd tasted just about everything the garden had to offer!

So, Lord,
   what can a father learn from all of this?
That children are inquisitive beyond belief?
That we can't be prepared for every eventuality?
That the diversity of nature is awesome?
That daydreaming can seriously damage your child's taste buds?
Possibly all of the above, but
   most of all, Lord,
   I have to admit,
   that, as a father, and admirer of nature,
   there is just one absolute certainty . . .
   Lord, I hate snails!

Cheesy, Spicy, Fruity Peaches!

A fruity number that can be served as a starter or a side dish or even as a sweet. Better still, enjoy it whenever you fancy something a little bit different on your taste buds!

Ingredients (serves 4-6)

150g/6oz mascarpone cheese
80g/3oz dark brown sugar
1 teaspoon cinnamon

2 x 400g/14oz cans peach halves
1 teaspoon freshly grated nutmeg
1 tablespoon lemon juice

1. Drain the juice from the tinned peaches and place peaches, cut side uppermost, in a large, shallow, ovenproof dish.
2. Place the mascarpone, cinnamon and lemon juice in a bowl and mix.
3. Put even quantities of the mixture in each peach half.
4. Grate the nutmeg over the mixture.
5. Place in a preheated oven, 200°C/Gas Mark 6, for about 20 minutes or until the cheese is nicely brown. Serve hot and smile.

Wooden it be nice!

Just a thought, Lord,
   but I did wonder
   whether you ever had a lapse in concentration,
   when you gave aunts the facility
   of independent thought?

I'm not criticising your creation, Lord,
   and I'm certainly not saying you left anything out,
   or left too much in!
But there are times
   when an occasional thought
   scoots across my neural sensors,
   wondering whether certain individuals
   should be left in charge
   of their own grey cells!

Now, ordinarily,
   I think gifts are something special,
   a treat, a token of affection,
   or just a way of saying thanks.
But what happened to the power of rational thought
   when a doting aunt
   lets a three-year-old boy
   have the run of the house
   armed with a carpenter's set!

On observing this act of generosity
   (isn't it fortunate that 'G' comes before the 'I' of idiocy
   in the alphabet),

I simply enquired whether one so young
could fully appreciate (or exploit)
the many uses of a carpentry set?
To be told that it might set the little fellow
on the straight and narrow,
to follow in the trade of one 'Joseph & Son',
carpenters to the stars,
simply begged the question
as to why anyone
in their right mind
would supply a hammer and saw
when there were so many curves around the house
to be put straight?

So, Lord,
while my son's favourite aunt
attempts an act of damage limitation
(she's trying to confine his architectural leanings to the coffee table),
I'm off to the local DIY store
to purchase a shelf-full of wood filler,
and some putty, paint, and a furniture catalogue
which, hopefully, will divert my son's attention
while his aunt checks out the cost
of replacement furniture –
that is, until our mutual friend
puts his carpentry set to one side
and drools over the pictures
of other household items that
require his attention!

Help . . .

Father,
   help . . .
Help me to see beyond my anger.
Help me to see above the issue.
Help me to understand . . .
   whatever needs to be understood.

Lord,
   help . . .
Help me to remember how exciting it was to be young.
Help me to remember how it felt to be wrong.
Help me to remember what sleep felt like!

Holy Spirit,
   help . . .
Help me to be patient.
Help me to see through a child's eyes.
Help me to be a dad!

Give me a break

Lord,
   give me a break.
This whole daddy business is so wearing.
I'm tired,
   I'm absolutely exhausted,
   I'm totally totalled.

Lord,
    give me a break
    from the continuous demands,
    the persistent noise
    of wants, tears, cries and chuckles.
The everlasting cleaning, washing and scrubbing.

Lord,
    give me a break,
    I just want to be normal,
    whatever that is!
It seems so long since our lives
    were transformed, changed or,
    to be more exact,
    altered beyond all recognition,
    into something that,
    to describe it, requires
    a lot of graphic language
    that would be more colourful than any rainbow!

Lord,
    my body aches,
    my head swims
    and my mind wanders.
My heart feels so heavy.
How can a little human,
    who is shown love and affection at every moment,
    demand so much of his parents?
There's hardly time to catch a breath,
    to think of anything more than our child's immediate needs.

It's almost impossible to plan ahead,
> other than have a sketchy idea of the contents for the next meal.

Lord,
> give me a break.

Give me a moment,
> give me a breath of time
> which I can call my own.

Where no demands clamour,
> or cries snatch at my conscience.

Where my needs,
> just for once,
> are all that need fulfilling.

Just for a moment, Lord,
> give me a break.

NURSERY NIGHTMARES

The moment you've been either dreading or wishing for has finally arrived. Now is the time for you to part company with your offspring and introduce them to yet another adult who'll have an influence on their life, the nursery teacher.

Now you will discover whether your innocent little creature will trash the nursery, inflict grievous bodily harm on the other little darlings or sit in the corner wondering why they've been abandoned!

Like it or not, this is a major event in both your lives. Will there be tears each morning as you walk, reluctantly, away from the nursery or will you skip down the path revelling in your newly acquired freedom? You also have the opportunity to chat to the other parents and discover that all those amazing things that your child can do is about average for that time of year! And, whether you like it or not, this is also the time when peer pressure and parental competitiveness loom large on the bank account. No amount of rational thought or economic logic will dissuade you from ensuring that your child must look as if they've arrived fresh from the fashion floor. Not only that, but your charming child will also choose the most embarrassing moment to drop some recently acquired vocabulary into a conversation with their grandparents!

First-day blues

While I wipe away a tear, Lord,
    spare a thought for this poor, unfortunate being.
My emotions are in turmoil,
    my stomach is as knotted
    as a macramé tea-cosy.
My eyes feel as if
    I've peeled a dozen onions,
    with my eyelids.

Lord,
    I'm not sure exactly how to feel.
Should I be in rapture
    at the amount of time on my hands,
    or should I feel guilty
    at dumping my responsibility
    upon someone else?

I'm not at all certain
    that I'm ready for this.
After all,
    it's not been that long
    since I was a totally inexperienced father,
    while now, well, I'm just plain inexperienced.

Surely I need longer
    to prepare myself for this educated separation?
I mean, let's face it,
    how can I expect some stranger,

    to recognise what a little genius they have on their hands?
Will they be able to appreciate the subtle charm of my child?
Do you think they'll realise that his refusal to do as he's asked
    is merely expressing his individuality?
Who will understand his preference
    to do exactly the opposite to everyone else,
    as a declaration of his democratic rights?

I'm sorry, Lord,
    but I'm not ready for this.
There's too much at stake,
    there's so much for me to learn,
    there's not enough preparation,
    not enough nurturing,
    not enough quality time,
    not enough development of a parental bond,
    not enough . . .
Excuse me, Lord,
    I'll have to get back to you on this one.
My little cherub has just thrown a paint pot on the floor . . .
Hey! Hang on a moment,
    do you think it looks a bit Picasso-ish?

Fruit and Nut Chocolate Extravaganza

It's about time to have something a little bit special! Not only is this treat easy to make, it doesn't need cooking!

Ingredients (makes about 20 generous pieces)
250g/9oz dark chocolate
25g/1oz butter or margarine
4 tablespoons evaporated milk
450g/1lb sifted icing sugar
50g/2oz roughly chopped hazelnuts
50g/2oz sultanas

1. You will need to grease, and dust lightly with flour, a 20cm/8-inch baking tin.
2. Place the crumbled chocolate, butter and evaporated milk into a bowl. Place the bowl over a pan of simmering water and stir continuously until all the ingredients have melted.
3. Remove the bowl from the heat and fold in the icing sugar.
4. Stir the hazelnuts and sultanas into the mixture.
5. Pour the mixture into the prepared tin, smooth the top and place into the fridge until firm to the touch.
6. Tip the cool mixture onto a chopping board and cut into squares. If you can resist the temptation to eat immediately, place the squares into paper cake cases and return them to the fridge until required. How long can you wait?

Myths, legends and suchlike

OK, Lord,
   here's a sticky one for you.
As you know, everyone likes a little bit of mystery,
   or something that seems to be a little out of the ordinary
     (no, I wasn't referring to my wife. Well, maybe not quite . . .).
What I mean is,
   as kids, things sort of appeared a bit special,
     kind of removed from the everyday tangles and boring stuff.
If something had a certain mystique or air of mystery about it,
   it acquired a touch of special-ness, out of the ordinary,
     something unexpected out of the cereal-packet job.

Finding some money under your pillow
   after getting a blister on your tongue
     through days of wiggling that loose tooth
        made up for all the hassle.
And Christmas morning
   wouldn't be the same
     without getting your own back on the birds
       by tearing and rustling every bit of wrapping paper
     as noisily as possible.
Even Mum and Dad
   made a special effort to get out of bed at 3am
     and politely suggest that a spot more sleep
       would help us to enjoy our presents all the more!

Now, here's where the sticky bit comes in.
I had no problem accepting that the tooth fairy

actually liked buying our teeth,
and that Santa really did like 250 glasses of sherry,
and several kilos of dodgy pastry filled with goo.
But, now that I'm the dad,
what do I tell the infant?
Do I suggest that they shouldn't sleep with their head under the pillow
just in case the tooth fairy gets greedy,
and that Santa's got a cholesterol problem?
Or do we really want to see Santa caught
for being drunk and disorderly,
in charge of a herd of reindeer?

Any advice would be extremely welcome.
Should I be politically correct?
Should I be biblically sound?
Should I be boring?
Or, should I be imaginative,
think like a kid again,
and enjoy creating the mystery?

Barking mad

Lord,
I don't know whether you can hear me very well,
it's a little bit muffled in here.
I'll just ramble a bit,
and hope that you catch enough of my drift
to make sense of things
(which is more than I ever will, that's for sure).

Thing is,
   I'm in the doghouse – literally.
The poor hound has been evicted,
   and I'm the latest resident of Chateau Pooch.
You just wouldn't believe that a simple fishing expedition
   could cause so much turmoil.

Just lately, we've had what you might call
   a lavatorial phenomenon,
   a kind of bathroom inertia.
You must know the kind of thing I mean,
   things were just not going the way they should!
It was nothing to do with eating more prunes,
   or dousing ourselves with syrup of figs,
   or even going vegetarian!

The problem, Lord,
   is simply that the toilet rolls are too absorbent.
Now, you might be wondering how fishing,
   vegetarianism and absorbent toilet rolls would lead
   to my current residence.

It all started the other morning.
Weaving my way to the bathroom,
   eyes sodden with sleep,
   I satisfied the commands of nature,
   flushed away the evidence
   and got wet feet.

There isn't a more certain way
   to travel from the natural state of slumber

to the widest awake there ever was,
than to receive a cold flood to the feet.

Grabbing the nearest implement that I could find,
   I hooked the toilet roll out of the loo
   (I wouldn't have minded so much, but it was a new roll!),
   dumped the soggy mess into the bath,
   squelched into our son's room
   and yelled something about the loo
   not being the most appropriate location for a toilet roll.

You can understand my son's look of amazement.
There he lay, staring at a loud Dad
   with wet feet, telling him not to put toilet paper into the toilet!
My wife, alerted to the fact that her male entourage were wide awake,
   appeared in the room,
   snatched her dripping toothbrush from my hand,
   cuddled our son,
   and told him not to take any notice of a grumpy daddy bear.
Sudden realisation spread across her face
   as she connected the toothbrush, toilet roll
   and shouting incident together.
I didn't hang around for the explosion.

So, Lord,
   here I am,
   at odds with my wife, son and dog,
   and hoping, sincerely,
   that you at least will talk to me,
   no matter how mumbled or rambling I may be.

Stir-fried Tofu with Peanut and Spring Onion Sauce

Providing you like tofu (bean curd), peanut butter and spring onions, you'll really enjoy this savoury snack.

Ingredients (serves 4)
450g/1lb tofu, cut into cubes
4-6 tablespoons (according to taste) crunchy peanut butter
1 teaspoon garlic puree
2 spring onions, finely chopped
150ml/¼-pint coconut milk
1 tablespoon tomato puree
1 lime

1. Dry the tofu while you heat some oil in a wok or large frying pan.
2. Cook the tofu for about 5 minutes. Once the tofu is lightly browned, remove from the oil and place on some absorbent kitchen paper.
3. The sauce is made by combining the peanut butter, coconut milk, tomato puree, garlic puree and juice of the lime together in a bowl.
4. Place the tofu onto a serving dish and pour the sauce over.
5. Sprinkle the chopped spring onions over the top and add the zest of the lime.

Cheers

Cheers, Lord,
    thanks and sorted.
Having safely returned
    from my sojourn at Chateau Pooch,
    I can't help but be thankful,
    that, no matter how much of a fool I am,
    or how much up to my neck in things I get,
    you're always around.

Even though
    I have to stand and account for my behaviour,
    or mumble an apology and offer a cup of tea,
    I know that you're there with me,
    possibly having a bit of a giggle,
    but at least you are there,
    whatever, whenever, whyever!

Cheers, Lord,
    thanks and sorted.

Transmogrification!

Lord,
    as you know,
    I'm a bit of an anorak
    when it comes to sci-fi and stuff.
The whole spacey bit really grabs me

TOOTHPASTE AND PASTA

(I was going to say abducts my senses,
but you might think that's corny),
and I like the scenes where things get changed, altered,
transmogrified!

It's different, unreal, imaginative and things.
Out-of-this-world stuff
   that couldn't really happen.
Well, that's what I thought until
   earlier this morning,
   as I ventured into the lounge
   in search of a bucket of caffeine stimulus,
   I met with a scene that would have sci-fi writers everywhere
   transfixed, amazed and even boggle-eyed.

All my senses told me that my surroundings
   were identical, or similar,
   to our lounge,
   but somehow, everything wasn't quite what it seemed.
A series of moving images emanated from one side of the room,
   while a sort of congealed substance spread itself across the floor.
A small being sat directly opposite the image transmitter,
   with a scent-impregnated cloth draped around its head.
From its mouth protruded a silica-based projectile
   which seemed to have a cloud of white foam surrounding its base.

Lord,
   I appreciate that this might sound slightly odd,
   surreal, or remotely weird,
   but, after a few neurons stirred within my brain,

NURSERY NIGHTMARES

I realised that this wasn't an intergalactic moment,
it was simply my son, watching TV
as the remains of his breakfast
lay abandoned at his feet,
while a face-cloth awaited his attention on his head
and he was playing silly games with his toothbrush.
Pretty normal stuff really,
don't you think?

Butter Bean Salad

This is a quick and easy snack that you can throw together in minutes.

Ingredients (serves 4)

2 x 400g/14oz cans butter beans, drained
200g/7oz feta cheese
2 tablespoons olive oil
2 teaspoons honey

3 spring onions, finely chopped
100g/4oz pitted olives (black & green)
2 medium tomatoes
1 tablespoon lemon juice

1. Place the chopped onions, olives and butter beans into a large bowl and mix together.
2. Cut the tomatoes into thin wedges and add to the mixture.
3. Mix separately the olive oil, lemon juice and honey.
4. Pour the olive oil dressing over the butter bean mixture and lightly toss the ingredients together.
5. Crumble the feta cheese over the top and serve.

Bugs and stuff

Lord,
    why do kids have this amazing ability
    to convert their tongue
    into a handkerchief?

What's so fascinating
    about this mucus stuff anyway?
It certainly doesn't taste very nice,
    or so I'm told!

Is the tongue-curling a genetic thing?
Or is it a conscious effort
    to seriously embarrass and annoy parents?
(Have you noticed that the number of tongue-wipes,
    is in direct proportion to the number of people around?)

Lord,
    I don't understand any of this.
I feel as if I'm wading through a mucus swamp
    (yeah, I've got a cold too);
    why do these bugs and stuff exist?
Are they a sort of biological mutation?
    'cos I certainly feel like a mutant of some sort
    when I've got a cold.

I have to admit, though,
    I feel kind of angry and irritated.
The irritable bit comes

as our young son whinges and whines,
   and does the tongue-curling stuff.
And angry at the fact
   that he's not well.

Lord, I feel frustrated,
     ineffectual, powerless to do anything
     that might do any good.
I suppose all I can do
   when he's feeling so rough,
    is give him a cuddle, wipe his nose
    and let him know that we love him.
Guess who we got that idea from?

Toothpaste murals

History is an amazing thing, Lord,
   it seems that the more we dig in the rubbish,
   the more we find out about ourselves.
Quite a philosophical thought really, don't you think?

I like watching those programmes on TV
    and wondering what the people were like
    who made weapons out of flint,
    and painted fabulous pictures on cave walls.

There always seems to be a mixture of the creative and the destructive
    in whatever we did, or do now.
Behind a perceived thing of beauty
   exists a collage of spoilage.

Is wreckage an intrinsic part of humanity?
Do we only begin to understand
   after we have taken life apart,
     molecule by molecule?

We appear to have an awesome capacity for destruction,
   and an ability to be ever more inventive.
Yet I still marvel at our ancestors' skill
   at creating so much with so little.

The thing that started my thoughts
   all began with the discovery
     of toothpaste graffiti in the bathroom.
Eccentric circles, lines, dots and squiggles adorned the walls,
   while the odd smudge on the floor
     lay as a testament to the artist.

Standing, smiling, still clutching an exhausted toothpaste tube,
   was our little creation,
     uncertain of our reaction to his endeavours.
Considering his ability to create so much from so little,
   his finger pointed to his art,
     he mumbled, 'My name' and I hugged him.

What else would you do?

PRIMARY PRANKS

The age of transition! After a few weeks, your offspring will begin to object to your holding their hand to school, grimace at the enforced kiss goodbye, and positively ignore you when their friends arrive.

This age seems to be a time of learning for everyone. Your child begins to learn about surviving at school; with a bit of education thrown in. There's the feelings of inadequacy, failure, peer pressure, time constraints, conflicting demands, and that's before you've even begun to give any thought to how your child is going to get on at school!

Now you begin to learn something about yourself. How will you respond to the demands of primary education? How will your child respond to you responding to them responding to school? A difficult time all round.

Scary teachers

It didn't seem so long ago, Lord,
    that we waved goodbye to our lad
      on his first day at school.
And yet, here we are again,
    waving with a tear in our eye
      (a cold wind blowing from the south!)
      wondering what kind of day he'll have.

On reflection though, Lord,
    is it really that we're concerned for our lad,
    or are we more concerned with how he'll behave,
    and how that will reflect upon us?
It makes you think.

As he wanders through the doorway,
    neat as they come,
    with monster-tread shoes
    that leave dinosaur prints wherever he walks,
    he scarcely looks back;
    almost too confident for his parents' emotions.
And we stare and think.

On reflection though, Lord,
    is it really that we're concerned for our lad,
    or are we more concerned with how he'll behave,
    and how that will reflect upon us?
It makes you think.

TOOTHPASTE AND PASTA

The day takes so long to pass
    as our lad experiences life in class –
    new friends and old friends,
    a new dragon to master
    with new routines to learn.
He's certain to make a few mistakes, Lord,
    but nothing that we can't get over.

On reflection though, Lord,
    is it really that we're concerned for our lad,
    or are we more concerned with how he'll behave,
    and how that will reflect upon us?
It makes you think.

Tagliatelle with Courgettes and Crème Fraiche

This is another quick and easy recipe that will impress your taste buds.

Ingredients (serves 4)

6 medium sized courgettes
5 tablespoons chopped basil
225g/8oz tagliatelle
Salt and pepper
1 fresh lime

4 garlic cloves, crushed
1 red pepper, chopped
150ml/¼-pint crème fraiche
2 tablespoons olive oil
6 tablespoons grated Parmesan cheese

1. Slice the courgettes into thin ribbons (a vegetable peeler should be OK).
2. Heat some oil in a frying pan and lightly fry the garlic.
3. Cook the tagliatelle in a large pan of lightly salted water and boil for about 10 minutes.
4. Add the courgettes to the garlic, and cook gently for about 5 minutes. Stir continually.
5. Stir in the basil, red pepper, crème fraiche and Parmesan cheese. Season with the salt and pepper.
6. Drain the tagliatelle, place in a warm serving bowl, drizzle the olive oil and juice from the lime over the pasta.
7. Place the courgette mixture on the pasta and serve immediately.

Thugs and mugs

I'm angry!
    Lord, I'm so annoyed.
I can't stand people who take out their insecurities
    on others.
It makes me mad, Lord.

I feel so powerless, Lord,
    to do anything about the hassle.
Why does some snotty little herbert
    think they have the right to act like a playground tyrant
    and run rings around those less thuggish than themselves?

I've been the caring, bearing parent.
I've said the 'There now, be brave' bit.
I've suggested making other friends
    and keeping out of the way.
But I'm now down to the 'Thump him anyway' strategy.

Lord, I must admit
    to feeling a little proud
    when our lad came home with a thick lip.
We asked him if he was OK,
    and he said, 'You should've seen the other kid!'

And now, Lord,
    I'm still so angry.
I'm downright mad.
We've just had a letter home, complaining about our little lad!

It seems we have some explaining to do
 about encouraging physical stuff.
Apparently, our little lad is now labelled the playground thug!

I'm just wondering here, Lord,
 about the right and wrong of it all.
It appears that whichever kid is the thug,
 it's the parent ends up the mug!

Education sucks

Lord, as you're the all-knowing type,
 and you've got most things sussed,
 it just occurred to me
 that you might like to have a word
 with those who make education suck.

I'm not talking about the teachers here,
 but those who say what to do.
They sit in their leather-backed chairs,
 spouting more hot air
 than all the hair-driers plugged into the National Grid.

They make judgements and decrees,
 produce statistics and lies,
 and expect everyone to be happy,
 with a formula that treats each kid the same.

Lord, I just want to say,
 that I think my child is different.

He's unique, like everyone else.
And I object to the pressure
   of learning to meet targets.

I feel under pressure,
   as if my child's success depends upon me!
And I'm made to feel guilty
   if we decide to play
   rather than study a word list
   for a test the following day.

It's no wonder, Lord,
   that the kids get a bit out of hand.
They're struggling to reach the targets
   set by people they don't understand.
And, Lord,
   when it comes down to it,
     I don't think I understand those people either!

I'm not sure that I want to ask for understanding, Lord,
   some things just seem too out of reach.
All I can ask, Lord,
   is that you help me
   to be there whenever our lad needs me.
To be around for him.
And, when he gets things wrong,
   not to try and measure him
   against a whole load of other kids,
   or make him feel that he's not up to the mark.
But to encourage him to do his best,

whatever that may be,
   irrespective of the statistics,
   the politics or targets.
Because, Lord,
   he's an individual,
   a gift, and we're proud of him
   just as he is.

Pear Tarts

This pudding takes a little bit of fiddling but the results justify the effort.

Ingredients (serves 4)

3 pears, peeled, cored and halved
25g/1oz dark brown sugar
25g/1oz pine nuts
250g/9oz ready-made puff pastry
25g/1oz butter
1 fresh nutmeg

1. Roll out the pastry and cut out six 10cm circles.
2. Place the circles onto a large baking tray (to make life easy, cover the tray with some baking paper).
3. Cream together the sugar, butter and pine nuts.
4. Place a small amount of the mix onto the pastry circle.
5. Slice the pear halves making sure that you keep the pears intact at the tip.
6. Place the pears onto the pastry circles and brush each pear with a little butter or olive oil.
7. Bake in a pre-heated oven, 200°C/400°F/Gas Mark 6, for 15-20 minutes, until the pastry has risen nicely and is golden. Serve hot with a sprinkle of freshly grated nutmeg.

The dentist

In your infinite wisdom, Lord,
    you decided, for reasons best known to yourself,
    to provide us with a constant reminder of our humanity,
    of our vulnerability
    to the microbes, organisms and other micro-wotsits,
    that somehow crept into your grand design.

They have an amazing ability
    to locate and inhabit
    all those little cavities
    that provide a home
    for vagrant food particles.

Lord, you must have known about this,
    the decay and black hole stuff.
But it begs the question,
    would there have been a need for a dentist
    in the Garden of Eden?

'Cos by my reckoning,
    if everything was perfect there,
    how could these micro-wotsits have existed,
    or found a vacant cavity?
So, was Adam's greater sin
    the fact that he never brushed his teeth between meals?

Let's face it, Lord,
    these enamel-coated bits

in our mouths
are a pain to get, a pain when you've got them,
and a real pain when they finally go!

I suppose they make eating a bit more interesting,
    because without them,
        we'd be sucking soup through a straw.
And, Lord,
    as you can see,
    I'm stumbling through these thoughts,
    here in the dentist's waiting room,
    while our lad sits reading comics,
    oblivious to what awaits
    beyond the waiting-room door.
As for me, Lord,
    I'm petrified,
    and I'm just visiting!

Origin of the species

It had to come, Lord,
    the question I've dreaded.
And, of course,
    one question leads to another,
    and before I know it,
    I'm up to my armpits in embarrassment.

I've sort of coped with the 'What's that?',
    'Why?' and 'Really!'

    but you can only go for so long
    playing parental ping-pong.
'Ask your mum', 'Ask your dad', 'Did you ask your mum?'
'Where did I come from?'
    seems an obvious question,
    and the answer, 'From Mummy's tummy',
    was bound to get the response,
    'How did I get there?'

Now, Lord,
    here's where I thought I had a flash of inspiration.
A visit to a farm,
    that's bound to solve the problem.
There you can see nature take its course,
    and the lad can ask the farmer all the questions
    I'm having trouble answering.

Well, I thought it was a good idea, Lord,
    but it has its drawbacks, as you now know.
He thinks that your surname is MacDonald,
    and, because Jesus was born in a stable,
    that's where we all start life!
I tried the 'Here's a chicken egg' approach,
    but now he thanks you every night
    that he didn't get eaten for breakfast,
    and he's off eggs big time!

And so, Lord,
    I'm sure that you're having a giggle
    at our embarrassment,

but I can at least thank you for one thing,
that you've given someone, at sometime,
a creative urge to draw a few pictures,
adding a few words,
so that I can buy the book,
nod wisely,
and point to the pictures,
and hope that our lad's reading ability,
is up to scratch!

Brussels sprouts and pasta

Lord, when you gave us freedom of choice,
    and the ability to make decisions
    for ourselves,
    had you ever considered
    school dinners
    before you granted us the delicacy of choice?

I thought at the time, Lord,
    that letting our lad have school dinners
    would solve the problem
    of the little chap falling headlong
    into his meal in the evening
    through sheer tiredness.

So, Lord,
    you can imagine our delight
    when, instead of choosing chips with everything,

the lad told us, with a certain pride,
that he'd had pasta for lunch,
with Brussels sprouts!

An odd mix, I know,
   but a good source of carbohydrate and fibre.
He told us he liked the pasta tubes the best,
   because, and we should have guessed the next bit,
   you can blow through them easily
   to play blow football with the Brussels sprouts!

It could have been worse, Lord,
   if he'd taken after me,
   he would have thought that summer pudding
   looked just like I imagined a plateful of sheep's entrails
   would have looked,
   swimming in custard.

I have to thank you, Lord,
   because without this lad of ours
   our eyes would have been dull
   to so many wondrous, childlike scenes.
And even though school dinners still make me cringe,
   at least they now make me smile, a lot.

Prawns in Tomato Sauce

A nice savoury treat that can be adapted to suit anyone.

Ingredients (serves 4)

450g/1lb peeled prawns
1 tablespoon tomato puree
4 cloves of garlic, crushed
6 fresh plums, chopped
1 onion, chopped

400g/14oz can chopped tomatoes
1 tablespoon brown sugar
1 teaspoon garam masala
1 tablespoon basil
Salt and pepper

1. Heat some olive oil in a large saucepan.
2. Add the onion and garlic and stir-fry for 2 minutes.
3. Stir in the garam masala.
4. Add the chopped tomatoes, tomato puree, sugar and plums. Bring gently to the boil, and then simmer for 6-8 minutes.
5. Add the prawns, salt and pepper to the mixture and cook for a further 2-3 minutes.
6. Gently stir in the basil and serve immediately in soup bowls.

SECONDARY SCARES

I really don't know why anyone calls this the 'Secondary' phase. You ask any emerging, or recently formed, teenager and they will tell you, this is it, life as we know it. It's quite simple to check this out. All you need to do is ask a teenager a question, any question. Now, wait a moment and 'Shazam!' there you have it, the answer.

This is the time that you should ask those questions that you've always wanted to know the answer to. Do it straight away, without delay. If you wait too long, and allow the teenage years to metamorphose into adulthood, the moment is lost for ever.

So much is happening during this time that it's difficult to appreciate the sheer amount of change that's taking place. The only certain thing in the whole process is that as your cherub matures, and reminds you of your grot years, your bank balance cannot keep up with the demands made upon it. Unfortunately, the phrase 'Can't keep up with the demands' is the excuse most frequently used by teenagers.

Hormone hell

Lord,
    I don't need a medical dictionary
    to tell me what is blatantly obvious.
This is an age when the chemical processes
    ravage the brain and turn our, once, little darlings,
    into pustule-infested psycho cases.

You can't ask them anything,
    you certainly can't tell them anything.
All innocent comments
    result in a verbal fallout
    that compares with a volcanic eruption,
    that burns our ears, and leaves a trail of guilt behind.

And, please, Lord, forgive me,
    but you'll have to remind me.
Was I ever young once?
I ask, you see,
    because, according to the all-knowing one,
    I don't know what I'm talking about.

Tantrums, slammed doors,
    threatening silences and beaming smiles
    are all too confusing
    after a day spent trying to understand
    the complexities of adult life
    as broadcast on daytime TV.

TOOTHPASTE AND PASTA

I'm looking to you for some divine inspiration.
A bit of help in these troubled years.
Because I seem to remember
 asking for help before,
  about how to cope with parents who don't understand me!

Coconut Pyramids

A simple snack, quick and sweet. What more could you want?

Ingredients (makes 6)
3 tablespoons self-raising flour
9 tablespoons sugar
350g/12oz desiccated coconut
3 eggs

1. Mix all the ingredients together and form into pyramids.
2. Place onto a baking tray.
3. Bake at 180°C/350°F/Gas Mark 4 for 10-15 minutes or until golden.

Is this music?

Lord,
   I feel so out of touch.
I've really lost it,
   whatever it was in the first place.

I thought I was one of those blokes
   whose finger was on the pulse.
You know, understanding and alive.
But now, Lord,
   it all seems very different.
I don't understand and there is no pulse.

I really do want to understand,
   to almost admit to liking some of the things I hear,
   but I have to admit
   that, try as I might,
   I just can't find a tune in the music they play.

Is it something to do with the ageing process
   that makes it impossible for me
   to understand a word that's being sung
   (and I use the word 'sung' to mean anything
   that's been ranted, spat or yawned)?
And, even worse,
   although the music is called 'industrial',
   is it meant to sound as if someone had recorded
   the sound of a production line
     making metal boxes?

Lord,
    you know I've tried.
I've listened, nodded and even tapped my feet,
    but, no matter what I try,
        it sounds as if I'm listening to someone dismantling a car
        with a sledgehammer.

The only conclusion I can reach, Lord,
    is to live and let live.
To hear and disobey
    that urge to pull the plug and hide the fuses.
The music isn't like the stuff
    that used to caress my ears.
And I have to accept
    that things have changed a bit
        since then.

But I think we can cope, Lord,
    as long as he plays his stuff
        out of sight, earshot and mind.
The only condition I make, Lord,
    is that whenever I'm driving the car,
        I play what I like, loud and in your face!

It's life, Lord!

Well, Lord,
    who would have thought it?
Here we are, parents of a streak of organic matter
    who's about to be launched on an unsuspecting world!

It seems minutes ago
    that we worried about his first pair of shoes,
    brushed his hair and straightened his jumper
    as he began his first day at school.

And now, here we are,
    worrying about how much more his feet will grow,
    when will he sort his hair out and wear a clean jumper
    as he's about to leave Secondary school.

In between then and now,
    many lumps and bumps, spills and thrills
    are etched in our memory and playing on our minds,
    and we wouldn't change a thing.

It's a minor miracle, Lord,
    how we've reached this place.
And we all know that without a bit of divine intervention
    the journey wouldn't have been quite so awesome.

Lord, there is so much to thank you for,
    yet so little I feel able to say.
I'm still feeling speechless and a bit out of breath,
    that this experience should happen to us.

Does it add up?

Is there a twist here, Lord?
I really can't make head or tail of this.
Because these fractions, formulae and equations
   just don't add up.

Whether it's a cosine, angle or degree,
   all seem to go off at a tangent to me.
The ratios and proportions, parallels and perpendicular,
   are approximately equal to nothing I understand.

If the square is the sum of two sets,
   and the triangle has a rank order lower than the mean value of one,
   how is a mere earthling father
   supposed to appreciate the finer things in maths?

If, by some chance of a miracle
   I was raised to the power of genius,
   by the simple inclusion of a square root,
   would I be able to help my son do his homework?

Maybe, Lord,
   I don't need an answer to this one, even if I could understand it.
I'm just so amazed that the human mind,
   having grasped the complexities of algebra,
   still manages to screw-up with such illogical behaviour.

Spicy Chick Peas with Ham

This can be a neat starter or a tasty snack. Whatever takes your fancy!

Ingredients (serves 4)
1 x 400g/14oz can chickpeas
3 cloves garlic, finely chopped
1 red pepper cut into strips
Olive oil

1 medium sized onion, chopped
200g/7oz ham, cut into thin strips
6 cherry tomatoes, roughly chopped
3 dried chillis, deseeded and finely chopped

1. Heat the oil in a large frying pan. Add the onion, garlic and red pepper, and cook for 2-3 minutes.
2. Add the ham and continue to fry for a further 4 minutes.
3. Add the chick peas, tomatoes and chillis, cook until thoroughly warmed.
4. Serve with a garnish of roughly chopped basil if required.

Perhaps?

Perhaps, Lord,
    it might have been easier on parents,
    and the world in general,
    if you hadn't put choice into everything.

There's so much of it around
    that I can't make a decision about anything.
Or can I?
I really don't know any more.
I sort of thought I'd got things sorted
    when exposed to the delights of the confectionery counter.
After years of chocolate choice,
    I decided to eat everything!

And now, Lord,
    choice just isn't simple any more.
Not when every advert, every magazine page and everybody
    screams that what we've got isn't enough or even 'in'.

But now, the constant moaning and groaning,
    the incessant nagging and grief,
    all because our boy's mates
    have got what he hasn't.

To him, we're just terrible parents,
    absolute horrors of the worst kind.
We obviously don't understand or appreciate
    that he's an outcast, a fashion leper.

TOOTHPASTE AND PASTA

Lord, I hope you're with me on this one.
But hasn't choice just made it difficult to be human?
I mean, if there's more than one of something,
   then you're going to get verbal abuse.

If you're not keeping up with the game, and wearing what's what,
   you get abuse from your mates.
If, as a parent, you're not throwing folding money into every store,
   you get abuse from your children.

I've tried the 'There's poor kids out there
   who would welcome your rejects',
     only to receive a hastily wrapped parcel
     and be told that now our child's got nothing to wear.
I'm expected to pay the postage too!

I've tried explaining what the prophets of old used to wear,
   and extol the merits of sackcloth and ashes.
Only to be told how weird I am,
   and that goatskin just wouldn't catch on.

I'm just waiting for the day, Lord,
   when sports shops and fashion are considered old hat,
   and anyone with a social conscience
   will dress from a charity shop.

Until then I suppose,
   that, as the good, understanding parents that we are,
   we'll keep digging deep and paying the cost
   of choice and fashion and style and stuff.

The evolutionary grunt

Lord,
   it's come to my attention
   that evolution might not be so fanciful as we imagine.
But, before you sharpen your lightning,
   and practise a thunderous growl,
   let me explain a little more,
   and allow me to remain a living, breathing dinosaur.

Now, don't get me wrong,
   or misunderstand.
I'd like to point out that Darwin got mixed up,
   and may have been up to his neck in the primordial swamp.
But I think that there is a slightly alternative view of evolution –
   the 'Cinderella' version!

There is no 'missing link' or evolutionary 'bridge'.
Nor are there millennia of adaptation.
The origin of the species emerges sometime before nightfall,
   knuckles scraping along the floor,
   hair sprouting from every pore,
   eyes sunk into the head,
   and a noise escaping from tightly scrunched lips –
   it's the evolutionary grunt of youth.

This 'evolutionary miracle' takes several hours,
   and the transformation is amazing.
Within minutes the knuckles leave the floor,
   the eyebrow ridges begin to disappear,

eyes emerge from the dark recess of the skull,
and the first word is spoken: 'Ugh'.

By the time night arrives
   the evolutionary animal has acquired a range of social skills
   that initially appeared impossible.
From 'ugh' to 'ergh' and on to 'aargh',
   the creature purses its lips and emits sounds
   that are almost understandable!

Unfortunately, this state of evolutionary development
   doesn't quite have a permanent state,
   the steps from 'aargh' to 'Hello, Dad',
   although a mere few hours evolving, are short lived.
As night thickens and the morning light threatens,
   our son degenerates into the creature from the swamp.

After a while, Lord,
   you sort of get used to the sight of primeval man.
You begin to accept the fact that your child rivals a sloth
   in its ability to hang around like a giant hair-ball.
The most worrying thing about this whole state of affairs, Lord,
   is that I'm beginning to understand what each grunt means
   and reply with a similar grunt!

Life, the universe and growing up

As we reach this stage of our family life, Lord,
   it's impossible to think
   that we've been able to get this far
   without a great deal of help from the Father of all.

At times, we've wondered
   why we ever conceived the idea of conceiving at all.
But, then again, our lives just wouldn't have been the same.
Less stressful perhaps, but not the same.

Even though, Lord,
   there have been times when it seemed
   as if we'd reached the end of the universe,
   and were in danger of disappearing into a black hole,
   a desperate cry for help has seen you surround us with hope.

I know that this is only part of it all,
   and that there is so much more to come.
But at least we can say we've been there,
   even if we've no idea how we got here in the first place.

As we look ahead, at life beyond the classroom,
   more education, employment and affairs of the heart,
   we can look forward with at least one confident thought,
   that you'll be with us throughout.

Thanks, Lord,
   for all that you've done, and all that we know you'll do.

We can only guess at what's to come, and what we'll have to face.
But one thought keeps us going, and that's what makes me smile,
  because when our children become parents themselves,
   it'll be time for grandparents' revenge!

Croissants Stuffed with Apple Puree and Yoghurt

This is just a quick 'fill-a-gap' snack that doesn't require much thinking about other than how many croissants to eat!

Ingredients (serves 2)
6 croissants
225g/8oz apple puree
350ml/12fl oz thick-set yoghurt
1 teaspoon cinnamon

1. Cut the croissant almost in half (widthways).
2. Warm the croissant under the grill.
3. Add a tablespoon of apple puree and top with a tablespoon of yoghurt.
4. Sprinkle cinnamon over the yoghurt.
5. Eat before the yoghurt melts!